AF429907

THIS JOURNAL BELONGS TO
THE BADASS:

____

CONTENTS

CONTENTS

Pages	Subjects

Pages	Subjects

www.ingramcontent.com/pod-product-compliance
Lightning Source LLC
Chambersburg PA
CBHW031738150726
47989CB00006B/2509